BOXE

A BOOK OF 21 PC

M000013681

BROWNTROUT PUBLISHERS
SAN FRANCISCO • CALIFORNIA

BROWNTROUT PUBLISHERS

P. O. BOX 280070 • SAN FRANCISCO • CALIFORNIA 94128-0070
800 777 7812 • www.browntrout.com

ISBN: 1-56313-914-6

BROWNTROUT publishes a large line of calendars, photographic books, and postcard books.
Please write for more information.

Printed in the U.S.A. by Chess Press
4977D Allison Parkway • Vacaville, California 95688 • 800 950 7812 • www.chesspress.com

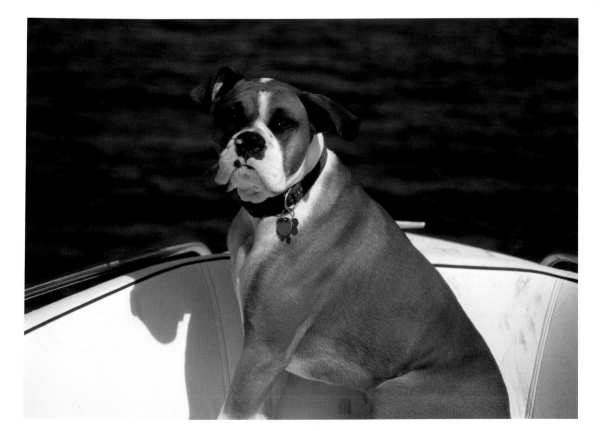

BOXERS

"The poor dog, in life the firmest friend
The first to welcome, foremost to defend."
—LORD BYRON

PUBLISHED BY BROWNTROUT • SAN FRANCISCO, CALIFORNIA

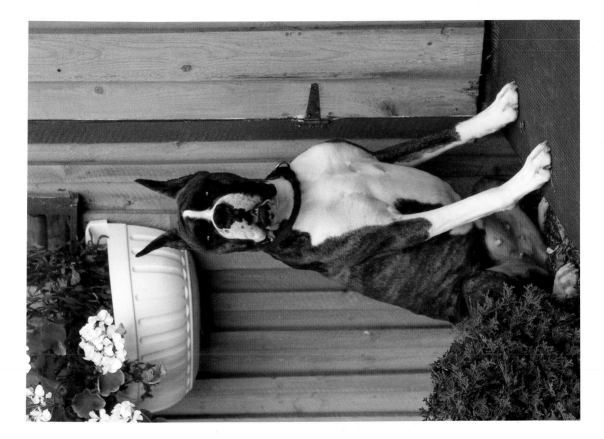

BOXERS

" 'Tis sweet to know there is an eye will mark
Our coming and look brighter when we come." —LORD BYRON

PUBLISHED BY BROWNTROUT • SAN FRANCISCO, CALIFORNIA

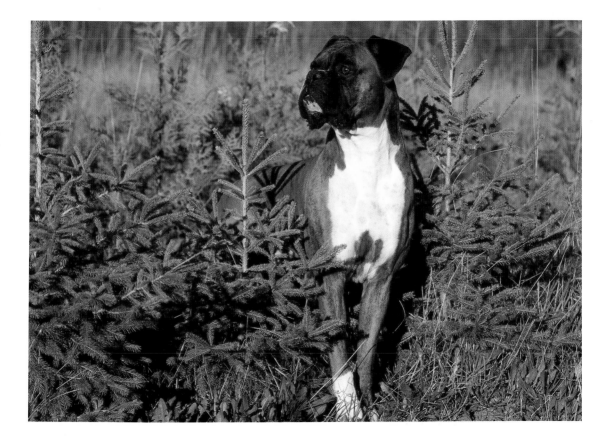

BOXERS

"Loving friend, the gift of one / Who her own true faith has run
Through thy lower nature, / Be my benediction said
With my hand upon thy head, / Gentle fellow-creature!"

—ELIZABETH BARRETT BROWNING

PUBLISHED BY BROWNTROUT • SAN FRANCISCO, CALIFORNIA

BOXERS

"The great pleasure of a dog is that you may make a fool of yourself with him and not only will he not scold you, but he will make a fool of himself too."
—SAMUEL BUTLER

PUBLISHED BY BROWNTROUT • SAN FRANCISCO, CALIFORNIA

BOXERS

"They are better than human beings, because they know but do not tell."
—EMILY DICKINSON

PUBLISHED BY BROWNTROUT • SAN FRANCISCO, CALIFORNIA

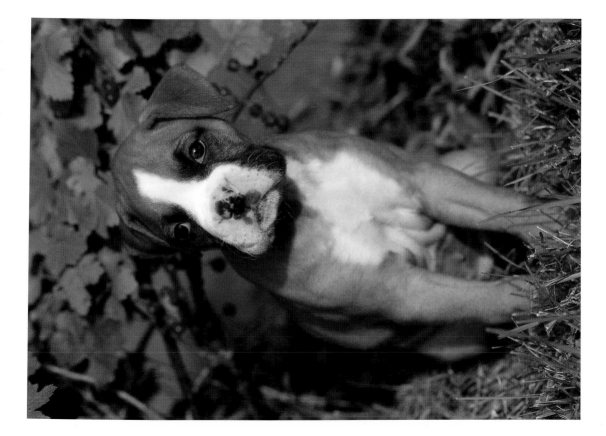

BOXERS

"…he will be our friend for always and always and always."

—RUDYARD KIPLING

PUBLISHED BY BROWNTROUT • SAN FRANCISCO, CALIFORNIA

BOXERS

"The dog was created specially for children. He is the god of frolic."
—Henry Ward Beecher

PUBLISHED BY BROWNTROUT • SAN FRANCISCO, CALIFORNIA

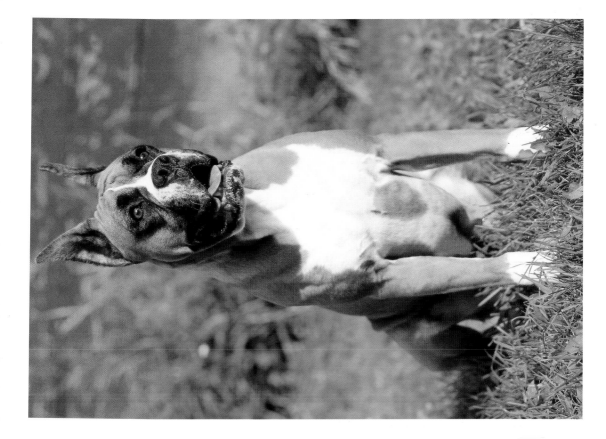

BOXERS

"Qui me amat, amat et canum meum." —St. Bernard

PUBLISHED BY BROWNTROUT • SAN FRANCISCO, CALIFORNIA

BOXERS

"Dog. A kind of additional or subsidiary deity designed
to catch the overflow and surplus of the world's worship."

— AMBROSE BIERCE

PUBLISHED BY BROWNTROUT • SAN FRANCISCO, CALIFORNIA

BOXERS

"In the concurring opinion of the wise, a dog, thankful for his food,
is more worthy than a human being who is devoid of gratitude."   —SA'DI

PUBLISHED BY BROWNTROUT • SAN FRANCISCO, CALIFORNIA

BOXERS

"Dogs are indeed the most affectionate
and amiable animals of the whole brute creation." —EDMUND BURKE

PUBLISHED BY BROWNTROUT • SAN FRANCISCO, CALIFORNIA

BOXERS

"The more I see of men, the more I admire dogs." —Madame de Sévigné

PUBLISHED BY BROWNTROUT • SAN FRANCISCO, CALIFORNIA

BOXERS

"I agree with Agassiz that dogs possess something very like a conscience."
— CHARLES DARWIN

PUBLISHED BY BROWNTROUT • SAN FRANCISCO, CALIFORNIA

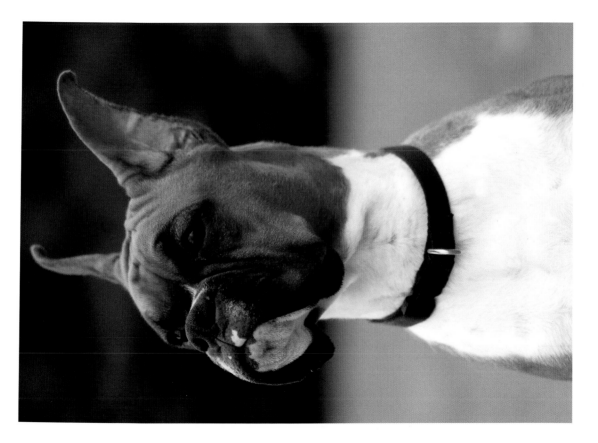

BOXERS

"The Almighty, who gave the dog to be the companion of our pleasures and toils, hath invested him with a nature noble and incapable of deceit."

—SIR WALTER SCOTT

PUBLISHED BY BROWNTROUT • SAN FRANCISCO, CALIFORNIA

BOXERS

"I would rather see a portrait of a dog that I know, than all the allegorical paintings in the world."   –Samuel Johnson

PUBLISHED BY BROWNTROUT • SAN FRANCISCO, CALIFORNIA

BOXERS

"A dog will never forget the crumb thou gavest him." —SA'DI

PUBLISHED BY BROWNTROUT • SAN FRANCISCO, CALIFORNIA

BOXERS

"Here, gentlemen, a dog teaches us a lesson in humanity."

—Napoleon Bonaparte

PUBLISHED BY BROWNTROUT • SAN FRANCISCO, CALIFORNIA

BOXERS

"Don't keep your dog always on a leash
if you want him to be attached to you." —A. WILLEMETZ

PUBLISHED BY BROWNTROUT • SAN FRANCISCO, CALIFORNIA

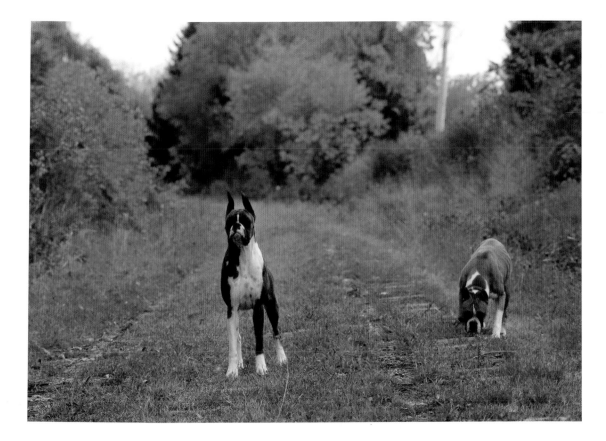

BOXERS

"Histories are more full of examples of fidelity of dogs than of friends."
—ALEXANDER POPE

PUBLISHED BY BROWNTROUT • SAN FRANCISCO, CALIFORNIA

BOXERS

"A good dog deserves a good bone." —BEN JOHNSON

PUBLISHED BY BROWNTROUT • SAN FRANCISCO, CALIFORNIA

BOXERS

"The dog represents all that is best in man." —Étienne Charlet

PUBLISHED BY BROWNTROUT • SAN FRANCISCO, CALIFORNIA